# Down on the Farm

# FISH

Sally Morgan

QEB Publishing

First published in the United States by
QEB Publishing, Inc.
23062 La Cadena Drive
Laguna Hills, CA 92653

www.qeb-publishing.com

Library of Congress Control Number: 2007001549

ISBN 978 1 59566 388 7

Written by Sally Morgan
Designed by Tara Frese
Editor Corrine Ochiltree
Picture Researcher Nic Dean
Illustrations by Chris Davidson

Publisher Steve Evans
Creative Director Zeta Davies
Senior Editor Hannah Ray


Printed and bound in China

## Picture credits

Key: t = top, b = bottom, c = center,
l = left, r = right, FC = front cover

**Alamy** / Jerome Yeats 14, Profimedia International
s.r.o. 18 tl; **Ardea** / John Daniels 6, Keb Lucas 7, John
Swedberg 12, Pat Morris 17 tl; **Barn Goddess
Fainters** / Stephanie Dicke 17 bl; **Corbis** / Carlos
Barria/Reuters title page 1, Clouds Hill Imaging Ltd 8
tl, Suthep Kritsanavarin/epa 19; **Ecoscene** / Robert
Pickett 8 cb, Peter Hulme 10, Reinhard Dirscherl 16 tr;
**FLPA** / Reinard Dirscher 4, Bill Broadhurst 5, Norbert
Wu/Minden Pictures 9, David Hosking 11, Frank W.
Lane 16 br, Wil Meinderts/Foto Natura 17 br; **Mik
Gates** 13, 18 br; NHPA 22.

# CONTENTS

Words in **bold** can be found in the Glossary on page 22.

# Fish on the farm

Did you know that fish give us meat, oil, and even eggs to eat? Fish are animals that live in water. They live in seas, lakes, and rivers all over the world.

This large fish is a carp. Carp live in freshwater lakes and rivers.

**FARM FACT**
A rainbow trout gets its name from the many different colors of its **scales**— blue, pink, yellow, green, and silver.

Some types of fish, such as carp, trout, salmon, sea bass, cod, and tilapia are raised in special fish farms. Fish farms can be based at sea or on land. Sea fish farms keep the fish in huge cages in the water. Fish farms on land keep the fish in large ponds.

5

# Fish from mouth to tail

Fish have **fins** instead of arms and legs. They use their fins and tail to swim easily through the water. They do not have lungs like us, instead they breathe using **gills**.

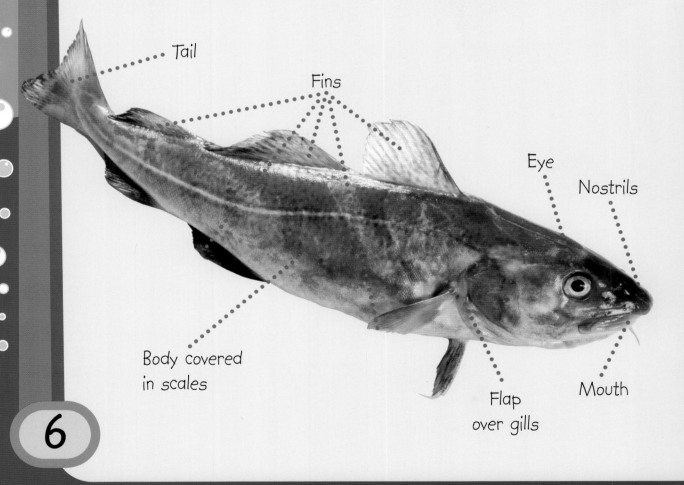

Tail

Fins

Eye

Nostrils

Body covered in scales

Flap over gills

Mouth

Fish come in different sizes.
An Atlantic salmon from a fish
farm can weigh 20 lbs. (9 kg),
but most weigh about 9–11 lbs.
(4–5 kg). That is the same as
four or five bags of sugar. These
salmon grow up to 5 ft. (1.5 m) long.
Farmed trout are smaller. They can
grow up to 29 ¹/₅ in. (75 cm) and
weigh up to 2.2 lbs. (1 kg).

This spotty
fish is a trout.

Size of a
six-year-old child

Size of a salmon

## FARM FACT
The world record for
the largest Atlantic salmon
caught on a fishing rod was
79.12 lbs. (35.89 kg). That's
about the weight of two six
year-olds. Now that's a big
fish! It was caught in the
Tana River, in Norway.

# It's a fish's life...

Trout begin their lives when the female fish lays her eggs. A tiny fish grows inside each egg. After a few weeks, mini fish called **fry** push out of the egg. They hide among plants to avoid being eaten by other fish. After a couple of weeks, the fry start swimming and eating. They eat tiny pieces of food floating in the water.

Fry do not have to eat for the first two weeks of their lives. They are born with a ready-made meal in a special egg sac.

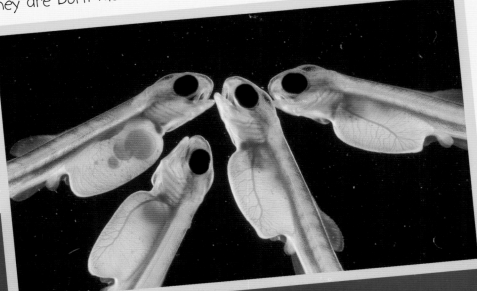

**FARM FACT**
Some wild trout
have been known
to live for up to
nine years.

Young fish that live on a fish farm
are fed special fish food every day to
make them grow quickly. They reach
their full size in just nine months. In
the wild, it takes two years for a fish
to become fully grown.

# Underwater life

Fish have to be kept in water to stay alive. In fish farms, they are given food that has lots of **nutrients** in it to keep them healthy.

This man is feeding fish in a fish farm.

Fish farms on land have different ponds for the fish to live in. These fish always have clean, fresh water to swim around in. Clean water pours into the ponds while the dirty water is taken away. The fish are moved from pond to pond as they get larger.

# Fish for food

Millions and millions of fish are eaten by people each year. Most are caught in the wild, but a quarter of all fish that are eaten around the world come from fish farms. This helps to protect wild fish numbers. When the farmed fish are big enough, they are caught in nets and taken to fish markets to be sold.

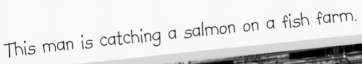
This man is catching a salmon on a fish farm.

Fish don't really have fingers! The finger shapes are cut from the tasty meat of cod or a fish called a hoki.

FARM FACT
One of the most expensive foods in the world is caviar. This is the raw eggs from a fish called the sturgeon.

Do you like fish fingers or fish and chips? There are lots of different ways of cooking fish. It can be **grilled**, **baked**, fried, and some fish can even be eaten raw.

13

# Eat fish, be brainy!

The meat of fish, such as trout and salmon, contains a lot of oil. Fish oil is very good for us because it contains lots of **vitamins**. The oil helps our bodies to stay healthy. It also keeps our bodies bendy because it oils all of our **joints**.

Cod-liver oil comes in little capsules.

This colorful fish is a rainbow trout.

This spotty, silver fish is a salmon.

Fish oil also contains something called omega-3. Omega-3 helps to keep our heart healthy and it is also good for our brain. So, what are you waiting for? Eat up!

15

# Fishy friends

## COD

The largest cod ever caught weighed an incredible 211.6 lbs. (96 kg). That's the same as three six-year-old children! Cod have a thick, hair-like organ sticking out from the bottom of their chin. This is called a barbel and they use it to taste things.

## TILAPIA

Wild tilapia live in rivers and lakes in Africa. They are farmed in Africa and parts of Asia. Wild tilapia females are great mothers. They look after their young by guarding their eggs and caring for the fry when they hatch.

## HALIBUT

The halibut is a large, flat fish. Imagine a fish that has been squashed completely flat— that's a halibut! Its fins are found along the edge of its body and both its eyes are on the top of its head!

## CARP

The carp is a large fish that comes from Asia. It has been grown in fish farms for more than 1,000 years. It is a cousin of the Koi carp that are kept in garden ponds all around the world.

# Fish around the world

## GERMANY

In many European countries, such as Germany, it is **traditional** to eat carp on Christmas Eve. The carp is eaten with potato salad.

## FRANCE

Around the world, April 1st is celebrated as April Fools' Day. In France, children stick paper fish onto their friends' backs as a joke. A person with a fish on their back is called a "poisson d'Avril"—an April fish!

18

## THAILAND

In Thailand, the giant catfish is thought to be a special fish. Eating its meat is supposed to bring good luck. Each year, fishermen hold a special **ceremony** to ask the river god for permission to catch the fish. Just look at the size of this one!

19

# A fishy mobile

Make a colorful fish mobile and hang it in a window. You will need a pencil, ruler, colored cardstock, scissors, fish pictures, white cardstock, crayons, glitter, sequins, and wool.

**1** Cut out a circle of cardstock that is 8 in. (20 cm) wide. Ask an adult to make six small holes around the edge. Add another hole in the middle of the circle.

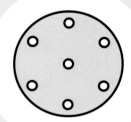

**2** Draw six different fish shapes onto cardstock. Have an adult cut them out.

**3** Ask an adult to make a small hole at the top of each fish. Color both sides with bright colors and draw the eyes and mouth. Add sequins or glitter for super shiny scales.

20

**4** Cut six pieces of wool, all different lengths between 11 in. (30 cm) and 20 in. (50 cm).

**5** Tie one end of a length of wool to a fish. Push the other end through one of the holes around the edge of the card circle. Tie a knot in the end of the wool so that it cannot slip back through the hole. Do this for each fish.

**6** Cut another length of wool to hang up your mobile. Tie a knot in one end. Thread the wool through the center hole. Hang your mobile in a window to catch the light and the breeze, and watch it sparkle.

21

# Glossary and Index

**baked** cooked in an oven

**ceremony** an event or performance to mark a special occasion

**fins** parts of a fish that are used to swim and for balance

**fry** the name given to a newly hatched fish

**gills** the parts of a fish's body that it uses to breathe

**grilled** cooked over a fire or under a grill

**joints** places in the body where two bones meet, for example the elbow, knee, and shoulder

**nutrients** nutrients are found in food. Our bodies need them to grow strong and healthy.

**scales** small, stiff flakes that cover a fish's body

**traditional** a custom or way of doing something that is passed from parent to child

**vitamins** our bodies need these substances in very small amounts for good health

23

# Ideas for teachers and parents

- Visit a fish market to see the range of fish on sale. See if you can find out which fish have come from fish farms and which have been caught in the wild.

- Look for some interesting fish recipes in a cookbook and help the children make the dish.

- Visit a trout or salmon farm. Many fish farms have open days when members of the public can visit. Open days allow children to see all the stages in the life cycle of the fish.

- Make a collage of a fish. Take a large piece of white paper and draw the outline of a fish on it. Look through old magazines and cut out any pictures of fish and fish-related subjects. Stick these within the outline to make a big, colorful fish.

- Visit a public aquarium to see all sorts of fish close-up.

- Buy a whole trout. See if the children can identify all the different parts of the fish. Look for the nostrils, mouth, eyes, gills, and fins. Use a knife to remove some scales and look at them using a magnifying glass. Ask the children how the fish moves through water. Remove the gill cover and look at the red gills underneath. Explain to the children that the gills help the fish breathe in water.

- Make a word search using the fish-related vocabulary in this book.

- Read about the different types of fish. Make fact sheets about them. Find out whether they live in the sea, rivers, or lakes, and what they eat.

- Ask the children to think of jokes and stories about fish. See if they can write a poem or a short story about a fish.

PLEASE NOTE
Check that each child does not have any food intolerances before eating any fish or making any dishes that contain fish.